10 Keys to
SUCCESS

PATRICIA KING

Published and distributed by:

XP Publishing
A Department of XP Ministries
PO Box 1017
Maricopa AZ 85139
patriciakinglifecoach.com

ISBN: 978-1-621660-84-2

10 KEYS TO SUCCESS
TABLE OF CONTENTS

FOREWORD

KEYS TO SUCCESS is a compelling look at God's precious pearls of wisdom. Patricia King has skillfully presented her readers with clear, concise, and convincing information that coaches, equips, trains, and propels hungry hearts toward their innate and inherent desires, dreams, and personal passions.

I have had the opportunity to serve Patricia as her Transformational Life Coach and have learned that she is a true ambassador of the Kingdom of Heaven. Her assignments are varied and vast, her mission is critical and with purpose, and her heart is to prepare a people of power and praise. While endeavoring to equip the 'whosoevers' to manifest the empowered life of an overcomer, she also challenges her readers to new heights in their spiritual ascent. She is truly an expression of the love and heart of God, and communicates triumph of achievement through the revelations presented in the *Keys to Success.*

I am impressed by the words of the famous football coach, Mr. Vince Lombardi, who said, "Leaders aren't born, they are made," just like everything else, through hard work. This is the price to pay to achieve your goals in life.

I encourage earnest readers who desire a positive change for their life to use *Keys to Success* to open all the effectual doors set before them. These doors can lead to the fulfillment of those God-inspired dreams, visions, prosperity, and legacy.

The activation of your keys to success comes through discipline, structure, and focus.

Remember, not to decide is a decision. Choose to embrace the procedure to change.

Please don't lose your keys!

Dr. Clarice Fluitt

President and Founder,
Clarice Fluitt Ministries

Co-Founder and Co-Pastor,
Eagles Nest World Prayer and Training Center

CEO, The Gennao Group International

Certified Transformational Personal and Executive Coach

Part One

God's Will for You
Is Success!

God's Will for You Is Success!

According to a Dictionary Definition, Success Is:

1. The favorable or prosperous completion of attempts, projects, or endeavors.

2. The attainment of wealth, position, honor, accomplishments, and fruitfulness.

Many people equate success with financial success but it is much more than that. God's plan is for you to "prosper and be in health, even as your soul prospers" (3 John 2 KJV). He wants you to succeed in every aspect of your life – every project, every endeavor! He wants you to be fruitful and to increase and multiply in every good thing. This brings glory to Him.

YOU ARE BLESSED — EMPOWERED TO SUCCEED!

In the very beginning, God BLESSED mankind. To bless means: to invoke favor upon and to empower to prosper (or it could mean, "empowered to succeed").

This is GOOD NEWS! You are called into God's blessing and if God has blessed you, who can curse you?

To live blessed in the Lord creates the manifestation of success and fruitfulness in life. Let's look at what God proclaimed over mankind in the very beginning of time.

> God blessed them; and God said to them, "Be fruitful and multiply, and fill the earth."
>
> ### GENESIS 1:28

This is amazing! God invoked His blessing upon mankind immediately after He created them. That blessing gives you all the empowerment you need to succeed. You were not created for failure; that is why it doesn't feel right when you experience it, or when the fear of failure knocks on the door of your heart. You were created to be fruitful, to multiply, and to fill the earth with His glory and goodness. You were created to be blessed and to succeed in everything that pertains to your life.

You might say, "Yes Patricia, but you have not factored in the fall of man. Success was God's original intention but then man fell from the blessing."

Come on, my friend! Read the rest of the Bible! Yes, we blew it. In fact, we blew it quickly and horribly, BUT God put a plan into place that completely redeemed us from the massive mess. When you are in Christ Jesus, you are set free from the power and consequences of sin and the law.

> The law of the Spirit of life in Christ Jesus has set you free from the law of sin and death.
>
> *ROMANS 8:2*

Through Christ you are restored to the original mandate of God's blessing. You are empowered to prosper, and the best news ever is that you don't have to strive or labor for it. It is a gift!

Proverbs 10:22 says, "It is the blessing of the Lord that makes rich, and He adds no sorrow to it."

The word *sorrow* in the Hebrew means "toil" and refers to sweat, labor, and strife. The blessing of the Lord creates your success, but there is no toil in it for you. When you choose to enjoy the Lord and His amazing goodness and grace, you will succeed. You have been born into the Kingdom of God to be blessed, to prosper ... to succeed. This is your portion in Christ!

Jesus paid the price for your deliverance from everything that would create patterns of failure in your life. He took all your sin and failure and nailed it to the cross with Him. In exchange He gave you His righteousness and success. He cut an eternal, unbreakable covenant with God on your behalf. That's right!

A covenant is a legally binding agreement between two people or two parties of people. In a covenant, there are terms that have to be both met and kept in order for the covenant to remain intact. God's covenant is a covenant of blessing that offers everything we need in life. Our terms are to love Him with all our heart, mind, and strength, and to obey all His commands all the time.

You see, mankind couldn't even begin to successfully meet God's terms and, if there were any possibility at all that we could attain to the initial fulfillment of those terms, we certainly couldn't keep them for all eternity. When the terms and conditions of a covenant are broken, the

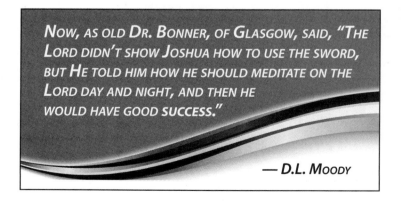

NOW, AS OLD DR. BONNER, OF GLASGOW, SAID, "THE LORD DIDN'T SHOW JOSHUA HOW TO USE THE SWORD, BUT HE TOLD HIM HOW HE SHOULD MEDITATE ON THE LORD DAY AND NIGHT, AND THEN HE WOULD HAVE GOOD SUCCESS."

— D.L. MOODY

covenant itself is compromised and as a result can be terminated. What a dilemma we were in! In fact, even today, if we in any way depend on our own righteousness and our own abilities to please God and keep the covenant, we will find ourselves in the same dilemma. It is impossible for us to accomplish the fulfillment of the covenant's terms.

Let's face it – we owed a debt that was impossible for us to repay. We were invited by God to fulfill a covenant we could never keep. He knew that and, as a result, in His great love for us He created a plan that is so brilliant, so amazing, and so outrageously good that it is actually hard to believe it with our natural minds.

He knew we could not meet or keep the conditions of the covenant so, in His great love for us, He humbled Himself and became man, fulfilling our part of the covenant! He fulfilled all the requirements for us to be free from the debt of sin and its consequences for all eternity. He hid our humanity inside of Christ's[1] perfection. When we come into Christ and Christ lives in us, we are one with the Perfect Man. He is now our life. Old things have passed away and all things have become new.[2] In Christ, God extravagantly gives us all the promises of

---

[1] *Christ* is not Jesus' name; it means "the Anointed One" and refers to His anointing. *Christ* means "the Messiah." Jesus IS the Christ.
[2] 2 Corinthians 5:17

13

His goodness and love in exchange for our sin. This is absolutely the truth!

Jesus is fully God and fully Man. He is the Perfect God and the Perfect Man, and has fulfilled the Perfect Covenant. This covenant can never be broken or tampered with by man's weaknesses, sin, or failures. You cannot break or weaken this covenant, because you did not make it, fulfill it, or keep it. He did!!! Hallelujah! Your part is to believe in Him and to receive Him as your God, Savior, Lord, King, Peace, Counselor, Provider, Healer, Deliverer, Wisdom, Strength and your All-in-All. Oh, this is so marvelous! He is everything you need.

Success has a name – JESUS! Oh, let's shout His glorious name for the entire world to hear. He is so GOOD!

Your success is assured when you give your life to Christ because His blessing in your life is sure. Your fruitfulness in every aspect of life has been purchased for you. It is your gift from your Daddy in Heaven who is crazy-in-love with you!

YOU ARE BLESSED!

As mentioned previously, to be blessed means to be invoked with favor and empowered to prosper. This is what you were created for. This is your portion in Jesus. Nowhere in the Scriptures does it say that those who belong to Him are cursed. You are blessed because you are in the Son! Jesus said, "The glory which You have given Me I have given to them" (John 17:22). He also said, "As the Father has sent Me, I also send you" (John 20:21). In the Father's eyes you are as Christ when you are in Christ and He is in you. God has exalted Him to the highest place and given Him all authority in heaven and in earth. And you are one with Him when you accept Him as your Savior!

In Christ, you are blessed beyond measure! You are blessed nonstop and continuously for all eternity! God's blessing over your life is like a river that never runs dry.

There is never a time that God says, *"I have changed My mind. I will only bless My Son fifty percent of the time. fifty percent of the time He will be blessed and fifty percent He will struggle. If you are in Him, you can expect only to be blessed some of the time – whenever I feel like blessing."*

NO! That is not the truth!!! For those of us who believe in Christ and have received His gift of eternal life by faith, we are blessed nonstop and continuously with every blessing needed to live an abundant life. The Word says so!

> Blessed be the God and Father of our Lord Jesus Christ, who has blessed us with every spiritual blessing in the heavenly places in Christ.
>
> *EPHESIANS 1:3*

> Grace and peace be multiplied to you in the knowledge of God and of Jesus our Lord;
>
> Seeing that His divine power has granted to us everything pertaining to life and godliness, through the true knowledge of Him who called us by His own glory and excellence.
>
> For by these He has granted to us His precious and magnificent promises, so that by them you may become partakers of the divine nature, having escaped the corruption that is in the world by lust.
>
> *2 PETER 1:2-4*

Whoo Hoo – this is exciting news. This is called the Good News of the Gospel! You have been delivered from every failure-producing curse that the fall of man created, and you have been brought into the fullness of Christ's blessing.

LET'S TALK ABOUT ABRAHAM

Abraham was divinely called to leave his family (living in the land of moon worshippers) and to follow God. God promised that if Abraham would follow Him, He would bless him. Genesis 12:1-3 spells out all the blessings God promised to give Abraham if he obeyed.

> Now the Lord said to Abram,
> "Go forth from your country,

And from your relatives
And from your father's house,
To the land which I will show you;
And I will make you a great nation,
And I will bless you,
And make your name great;
And so you shall be a blessing;
And I will bless those who bless you,
And the one who curses you I will curse.
And in you all the families of the earth will be
blessed."

In this prophetic word, God revealed His plan of salvation. Through Abraham's seed, the blessing of the Messiah would come. God promised personal blessing upon Abraham and on his descendants IF he believed and followed. Abraham did believe God, and he did follow. As a result, his faith was credited to him as righteousness, and the blessing came into the earth.

This is amazing. It was simple faith that caused Abraham to be the most blessed man on the face of the earth. Abraham was blessed every day of his life as he walked with God. There was never a time when he was not blessed. He faced famines and drought but they never touched him. He lived in times of war but he only knew the victory. He was successful and fruitful in all things. In fact, God even caused his mistakes to turn around for ultimate blessing.

For example, one glitch in Abraham's walk was when he chose to tell a half-lie as he entered into Egypt. He was afraid that they would kill him if they thought Sarah was his wife, so he instructed her to say she was his sister. But God turned it around for good. Once the situation was clarified, Abraham not only left Egypt with Sarah, but also with a great deposit of goods from the king. When you live in the blessing of God, even your disasters turn around for good.

Abraham lived in the supernatural dimensions of God's blessings, because of his faith, all the days of his life. His son Isaac came forth as a result of Abraham's faith. Both Abraham and Sarah were past their child-bearing years – way past! But Abraham continued to believe that his descendants would be as numerous as the stars in the sky. It seemed impossible in the natural, but he believed, and the supernatural blessing kicked in. There is nothing impossible for God, and Abraham believed that. He believed that he was blessed and never lost sight of it.

Later, God told Abraham to sacrifice his promised son Isaac, and because Abraham so believed in the goodness of God, he was willing to obey. He knew that God would either raise Isaac from the dead or provide a substitute. He believed in God's goodness.

Abraham believed in the goodness and blessing of God, and God saw Abraham's faith and said, "I am going to credit that faith as righteousness." God had promised him good things and he believed it. God said he would be blessed and he believed.

Abraham did not focus on his sin and failures but focused on God's goodness. When you focus on the perfection and awesomeness of God's goodness and blessing towards you, you forget about yourself and live in the grace of His glory. Abraham's faith in the promise of God's blessing was credited to him as righteousness, posturing him to succeed and live in the perpetual extravagance of God's goodness all the days of his life.

Even when Abraham was one hundred and seventy-five years of age, he was rich in all things. He never downsized or diminished in blessing. He continued to succeed in all things[3] for the entire course of his life. He never had a "bad year."

The covenant of blessing that God made with Abraham was the covenant of good news (the gospel) that we see fulfilled and sealed for all people and for all time through Christ in the New Testament. That is why Old Testament saints who believed in the Messiah prior to Jesus' finished work on the cross went to Abraham's bosom[4] when they

---

[3] Genesis 15:6

[4] *Abraham's bosom* was a heavenly state in Sheol that was separated from hell by a chasm. The righteous dead of the Old Testament who believed in the Messiah to come and the covenant of salvation went there when they died (see Luke 16:23).

died. They were saved even before Jesus ratified the covenant through His death and resurrection because they believed.

In the New Testament, Abraham is mentioned frequently to reveal to us our covenant in Christ. Look at this amazing word:

> Christ redeemed us from the curse of the Law, having become a curse for us – for it is written, "Cursed is everyone who hangs on a tree" –
> In order that **in Christ Jesus the blessing of Abraham might come** to the Gentiles, so that we would receive the promise of the Spirit through faith.
>
> *GALATIANS 3:13-14*

This is awesome! The blessing of Abraham, according to Genesis 12:2-3, is that we are blessed (invoked with favor and empowered to prosper) and are made a blessing, and nations will be blessed through our faith. We have the power and the mandate to fill the earth with the knowledge of the glory of God. You are blessed! You are empowered to prosper! You are created for success!

The empowerment to prosper is not given so that you can hold onto the blessing for yourself and operate in a withholding spirit. No way! You are empowered to prosper in order to bless others – in fact, you are called to bless the earth – its people, its creation and its nations. You are called to be fruitful and to multiply. Jesus took care of all the obstacles and now you, like Abraham, can live your ENTIRE LIFE in the blessing of God in order to fill the earth with His goodness and glory. You are destined for success in every area of your life. You are! God says so!

Abraham was successful in His relationship with God, in marriage, in family, in provision, in business, in battle, in land ownership and development, and in relationships. He was also blessed with angelic visitation and spiritual encounters. He was highly favored and empowered to prosper in *every* area of his life. Like him, you are called to live in that blessing of success. The New Testament declares it.

It gets even better!

Here is a portion of Scripture the Lord revealed to me during a heavenly encounter. Please don't read it quickly – it is too powerful to take lightly. Personalize it.

> He has made an everlasting covenant with me,
> Ordered in all things and secured;
> For all my salvation and all my desire,
> Will He not indeed make it grow?
>
> *2 SAMUEL 23:5*

These were David's final words. King David was actually a New Testament believer living in the Old Testament days. Through his writings in the Psalms it is very clear that he knew the Messiah, whom he called "The Lord," by faith.

David understood that he had an eternal covenant of blessing with God. In this Scripture verse, he describes the eternal covenant as the catalyst that caused his life to be **ordered** in all things and **secured**. Your life in Christ is divinely ordered. You have the power to call things in your life that might not be in God's perfect order into His order. Your covenant with God promises that your life will be ordered in all things and come into alignment.

David also revealed that the covenant blessings were **secured** in his life. God's chosen covenant is a secure thing that does not jump up and down like the stock market. It is the same for eternity – always good!

What we have just read is good in itself, but it gets even better. David said, "All my **salvation** and all my **desire**, will He not indeed make it **grow**?"

Salvation[5] in this context means: Deliverance, salvation, rescue, safety, welfare, prosperity and victory.

Desire[6] means: delight, pleasure and longing.

Grow[7] means: to sprout, spring up, grow up, to grow abundantly or thickly.

---

[5] Strong's Concordance H3468 *yesha*
[6] Strong's Concordance H2656 *chephets*
[7] Strong's Concordance H6779 *tsamach*

This is so exciting – I can barely stand it!

In this covenant of blessing, all your freedom, rescue, salvation, deliverance, prosperity, victory, longings and deepest desires will sprout, spring up, and grow up into abundance and thickness. This is the truth! Do you believe? If you believe it, you can have it!

In my book *Create Your World*, I share the importance of having core beliefs that are aligned with truth. When you have a strong standard of truth in your core, you will be immovable and unshakable, and the very things you believe will manifest in your life. When you establish core beliefs that are aligned with God's promises and truth, realms are created in your life that actually attract to you the very things you believe. This is very powerful – watch what you believe.

It takes time to establish new patterns of beliefs and eliminate deceptive "default beliefs" that can hinder you from your breakthrough but, if you lean on the grace of Jesus, He will empower you for the breakthrough with ease. Grace is undeserved, unmerited favor from God, but it is also His divine influence and power working on your heart and life. Jesus has made it so easy for you because He loves you! Keep your focus on Him and His goodness – He fulfilled it all for you.

In light of the promises contained in 2 Samuel 23:5, you can begin right now to decree blessings over your life. The Kingdom of God is "voice activated." When God created, He spoke things into existence. Your decrees of the words contained in God's covenant are powerful and they create realms of blessing. (To receive further empowerment, consider acquiring *Decree* and *Create Your World* featured in the Resource section in the back of this book.)

Here is a decree based on 2 Samuel 23:5 for you to proclaim over your life right now:

> God has blessed me with an everlasting covenant that has granted me divine order for my life in all things according to His good promises. Everything is coming into alignment to His truth, and every good thing that He has promised is secured in me and cannot be shaken. I fully trust God to keep the things that I have committed to Him. I am fully secure in the blessing of God for all my days. All my salvation and all my desire sprouts and grows into abundance. All that I am, all that I have, and all that I do is blessed.

Can you see yourself living in the fullness of a fruitful and successful life? Lock into this eternal reality – the promise is yours! You do not ever need to receive failure, because you are blessed with success – it is your gift, purchased for you by Jesus two thousand years ago.

The Bible is your handbook for life. In its pages you will find truth that will open up realms of success for you. Invite the Holy Spirit to open your understanding to the keys for success found within its glorious pages.

My popular coaching course, *KEYS TO SUCCESS*, thoroughly outlines ten keys discovered in the Word that promise success for every child of God. The course also includes effective activations to help participants get the message of success established in their lives.

Here in this companion book, Part Two gives you an overview of those 10 Keys to Success found in Scripture.

SCRIPTURES TO MEDITATE ON

GENESIS 1:28

God blessed them; and God said to them, "Be fruitful and multiply, and fill the earth, and subdue it; and rule over the fish of the sea and over the birds of the sky and over every living thing that moves on the earth."

NUMBERS 6:22-27

Then the Lord spoke to Moses, saying, "Speak to Aaron and to his sons, saying, 'Thus you shall bless the sons of Israel. You shall say to them: The Lord bless you, and keep you; The Lord make His face shine on you, and be gracious to you; The Lord lift up His countenance on you, and give you peace.' So they shall invoke My name on the sons of Israel, and I then will bless them."

PROVERBS 10:22 NKJV

The blessing of the Lord makes one rich, and He adds no sorrow with it.

DEUTERONOMY 28:2

"All these blessings will come upon you and overtake you if you obey the Lord your God."

DEUTERONOMY 28:8

"The Lord will command the blessing upon you in your barns and in all that you put your hand to, and He will bless you in the land which the Lord your God gives you."

JOSHUA 1:7

"Only be strong and very courageous; be careful to do according to all the law … do not turn from it to the right or to the left, so that you may have success wherever you go."

JOHN 10:10

"The thief comes only to steal and kill and destroy; I came that they may have life, and have it abundantly."

JOHN 15:7-8

"If you abide in Me, and My words abide in you, ask whatever you wish, and it will be done for you.

"My Father is glorified by this, that you bear much fruit, and so prove to be My disciples."

2 CORINTHIANS 2:14

But thanks be to God, who always leads us in triumph in Christ, and manifests through us the sweet aroma of the knowledge of Him in every place.

GALATIANS 3:13-14

Christ redeemed us from the curse of the Law, having become a curse for us – for it is written, "Cursed is everyone who hangs on a tree" – in order that in Christ Jesus the blessing of Abraham might come to the Gentiles.

3 JOHN 2

Beloved, I pray that in all respects you may prosper and be in good health, just as your soul prospers.

PART TWO

An outline of the
10 KEYS TO SUCCESS
THAT ARE STUDIED IN-DEPTH IN THE
KEYS TO SUCCESS LIFE COACHING COURSE.

KEY #1

T<small>AKE</small> I<small>NVENTORY</small>

As we continue to use Abraham as our example, we see that he was a balanced man – he had success in every area of his life. Other Bible characters, such as David, had success in many areas of their lives and yet had some blotches in other areas, as revealed in Scripture.

God is so forgiving and gracious that He will pardon and cleanse us from all unrighteousness when we confess our sin. He is enormously kind and merciful! David received the mercy of God, but his choices to walk outside of God's presence and ways created some big trouble… sin always will. It would have been so wonderful to see David's life blessed in every way. If he had taken inventory of his life, he might have realized that he needed to receive God's blessing of alignment into the area of marriage and family. He suffered much pain personally from the consequences of this arena of his life being out of balance and order, and so did the nation. The areas of your life that are not in order do not only affect you but those around you. The larger the sphere of influence you have, the more people can be affected either for good or for evil.

God wants you to succeed in every area of your life.

In our coaching course, *KEYS TO SUCCESS*, we invite the participants to take an inventory of the twelve main areas of their life and evaluate on a chart the success status in each area. It is enlightening to see it unfold on the graph. When you are able to see the bigger picture, it helps you to know what to believe God for, because God is committed to pouring out empowering grace upon you in every area of your life.

The twelve areas of your life that we examine in the coaching course are as follows:

1. Spiritual
2. Personal
3. Learning – Academics
4. Health/Fitness/Grooming
5. Financial/Possessions
6. Career/Work
7. Marriage/Single Life
8. Family/Children

9. Friends/Relationships

10. Home

11. Social/Recreation/Hobbies

12. Volunteer

Ask the Lord to help you succeed in every dimension of your life and to show you what area you need to work on first. A momentum of success will get established once you begin to take victories. One success will produce the next one, and the next one, until a realm of success is foundational in your life.

KEY #2

FAITH

Our study of Abraham in Part One clearly revealed that his success was based on his faith in the goodness of God. He believed God's promises and as a result was successful in every area of his life. In contrast, the children of Israel, in their exodus out of Egypt, chose doubt and unbelief. Like Abraham, they also had the promise of God, but they doubted His goodness every day. They failed to enter their promised destiny because of their hardened heart of unbelief. What a contrast between the children of Israel and Abraham! Faith in God's goodness and promises secures success.

Jesus said, "All things are possible to him who believes" (Mark 9:23). Jesus spoke these words in the midst of a dramatic situation. A man's son experienced seizures and he brought him to the disciples, but they could not deliver or heal him. Jesus told the father to bring the boy to Him and said, "All things are possible *to __him__ who believes.*" Who is Jesus referring to when He said, "All things are possible to him who believes"? The disciples did not have faith, the father did not have faith, the son did not have faith, so who is Jesus referring to? He was referring to Himself. All things are possible to Jesus because He has perfect faith.

When we are looking at naturally difficult or seemingly impossible situations, we must remember that all things are possible to Him. He believes perfectly, and His faith has been given to us. In Mark 11:22 Jesus said, "Have faith in God." The more accurate translation is, "Have the faith of God" or "Have God's faith."

It is important to believe in One who is greater than yourself. You were created by the all-powerful, all-mighty, all-righteous, and all-wise God who has invited you into an

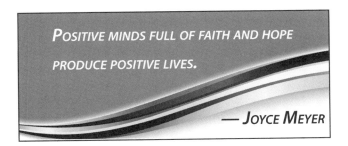

POSITIVE MINDS FULL OF FAITH AND HOPE PRODUCE POSITIVE LIVES.

— *JOYCE MEYER*

eternal relationship and partnership with Him through Jesus Christ.

In Part One we covered the subject of the eternal covenant of blessing we have with God. This covenant was given to us as a gift, and no effort of our own has ever been involved.

In Ephesians 2:8-9, the Scripture confirms: "For by grace you have been saved through faith; and that not of yourselves, it is the gift of God; not as a result of works, so that no one may boast."

Grace refers to God's blessing of unmerited, undeserved favor toward us and His influence upon our heart and mind. This Scripture reveals that we have been saved by grace through faith, and even our faith is a gift from God — it is not a result of our own striving and effort to believe. So, how does this work? How is faith produced?

When you gaze into the goodness of God, when you behold His grace and kindness, you begin to believe. You don't strive to believe, but you simply enter the grace. In His grace is the faith to believe; most of the time you aren't even aware of faith when it is operating because it is simply the result of gazing into Christ. Your faith is a gift found in His grace. If you are under legalistic oppression and believe that YOU have to obey the law in order to obtain favor from God, you will never produce faith and, therefore, you will never see the promises you long to fully manifest in your life.

Romans 10:17 teaches that "faith comes from hearing, and hearing by the word of Christ." The Greek translation of *word* in that verse is "rhema,"[8] which refers to a life-giving, Spirit-quickened word. Jesus stated in John 6:63 that the words He spoke were "spirit" and "life." Faith is produced by words that flow from His heart. His heart connection to your heart is by grace, not by works, and not because you have done anything to deserve it. When I draw close to the Lord and meditate on His amazing grace, unconditional love, and limitless goodness, I always hear Him speak to my heart. He speaks words of blessing, truth, comfort, and encouragement. Those are the words that create faith. The words that come from His grace create faith in us. When this transactional impartation takes place, we are not usually aware that we are operating in faith. We are simply absorbed in His goodness and grace, and faith is automatically in operation. We believe because our hearts are one with Him and His faith has entered us. That is the nature of His work of grace in us. In His grace is the gift of faith.

---

[8] Strong's Concordance G4487

If you remain in His grace, faith will grow, but you might not even realize it.

God sees your faith when it flows towards Him, but you usually only see His grace. That is all you need. You cannot strive to believe, simply be a gazer and a grazer on His goodness. This will create success in your life.

KEY #3

POSITIVE CORE BELIEFS AND VALUES

CORE BELIEFS

A truly successful person has strong, godly, core beliefs. You are what you believe. Your perspective forms and creates your life.

A number of years ago, I was listening to a woman share her frustration regarding her faith. She longed for a meaningful relationship with the Lord but testified that she felt distant and never fully accepted by Him. I began to question her regarding the foundations of her beliefs and discovered that she had been taught some religious and legalistic interpretations of Scripture that forced her into a performance mode. She never knew that salvation was a gift by grace, so she was always striving in her attempts to please God, feeling distant from Him and never worthy or loved. The reason this tormenting fruit was manifesting in her life was due to her wrong core beliefs.

That day she finally heard the gospel according to truth. Her eyes were opened to the revelation that Jesus accomplished everything for her on the cross two thousand years ago. She wept and wept, feeling His presence very strongly. What made the difference? Her beliefs had changed to align with truth.

Your success in life is based on your beliefs about God and about yourself. Believe the truth and you will prosper.

Jesus shared with His disciples that the Spirit would come and lead and guide them into all truth.[9] The Spirit of God is with you to lead you in the truth and keep you in the truth. He will only witness with the truth. If you choose to believe a lie, He will not agree with it. He will only agree with the truth. If you remain in the Word, He will confirm the truth to you and you will prosper.

God told Joshua to meditate on the word day and night so that he would have prosperity and success.[10]

The Bible is your handbook to lead you into success. Believe the truth within its pages and you will prosper.

---

[9] John 16:13
[10] Joshua 1:7-8

CORE VALUES

What are your core values? Your values mold your life. I know a man who is a certified public accountant. He values integrity and excellence. As a result, he has enjoyed a successful accounting career for years because his clients trust him. Even if he had opportunity, he would never be dishonest, because his core is established in integrity.

If you have weak and compromised values, you will default to them when you're in a hard, critical place. However, if you have strong values and solid convictions, that is what you will default to. Your core values are your default values.

A person who has solid, godly values will be favored by God and man. You can trust someone whose values are solid and full of integrity.

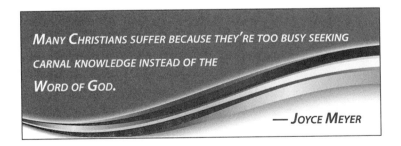

MANY CHRISTIANS SUFFER BECAUSE THEY'RE TOO BUSY SEEKING CARNAL KNOWLEDGE INSTEAD OF THE WORD OF GOD.

— JOYCE MEYER

I have a friend who has very clear moral boundaries established in her core. She desired to be married but she was not willing to compromise her core values concerning sexual purity. One time a man she was dating showed her affection that could lead to compromise. She immediately communicated her core values with him – it was not difficult because her default was established in her core. He was surprised because he had never encountered that level of moral integrity before, but he deeply respected and honored her for it. They developed a close, meaningful, and God-blessed relationship built on good core values and purity. Eventually they were engaged and then married. He was amazed at how deep and meaningful the relationship was able to go in the Lord when the physical and sexual draws were subdued. Strong core Kingdom values that actually opposed the values in the world made the way for this relationship to be successful and blessed.

KEY #4

CLEARLY DEFINED
DESIRES AND GOALS

You have been created in the image and likeness of God. It is important to have clearly defined desires, dreams, and goals. He did! For example, He had a clear desire, dream, and goal to redeem man from His sin. He was not nebulous regarding His purposes but had well-defined goals that He communicated all through the Bible.

God's goal was realized in the fullness of time through His amazing plan of salvation. What are your desires? What goals are you targeting? This is an important key to success.

Your D.R.E.A.M.s need to be:

1. **D**efined – clear, well defined and specific.

2. **R**elevant – relates to you, your life, your future.

3. Expected End – your dream has a clear goal or expected outcome.

4. Attainable – not a pipe dream but one that can be accomplished.

5. Measurable – you should be able to measure the results and fruitfulness.

Pursuing a dream takes risks and launches you into a journey of trust. The Lord will walk with you each step of the way and you will learn valuable lessons. If you do not dream and define goals in your life, you might drift through life and fail to accomplish many of the assignments the Lord has for you.

Successful people are dreamers. Successful people embrace the journey.

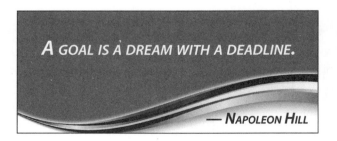

A GOAL IS A DREAM WITH A DEADLINE.

— NAPOLEON HILL

KEY #5

PASSION AND FOCUS

What are you most passionate about? If you can determine your passion, you will be able to identify the area of your life that you can be most successful in. As a Prophetic Life Coach, I enjoy helping people define their dreams and experience the fullness of what is in their heart. If I can help them identify their passion, I can usually help them move into success in that area.

Athletes know the power of passion and focus. When speaking with a sports trainer one day, I asked him what he believed was the greatest factor for success in athletics. He replied that it was undoubtedly the individual's passion. He explained that he had met many gifted and skilled individuals, but they always fell short of their potential if they lacked passion. Lacking passion, they failed to focus on practice and their game.

He further explained that he would rather work with a passionate athlete than a gifted or skilled one who lacked passion, because the passionate athlete with focus and perseverance could develop the skills and break through into a realm of excellence. He emphasized that the very best case scenario is to find an individual who was both gifted and filled with passion and focus.

Successful individuals are usually full of passion that motivates them to focus and fulfill their dreams, visions, and desires.

Whatever you focus on, you will ultimately empower in your life.

I am personally not a multitasker. My mind does not focus on two things at the same time, and it is actually impossible to give two things full focus at the same time. I am not saying that you cannot be aware of more than two things at a time, but you cannot give your full focus to more than one thing at any given moment. Full focus is very powerful. Successful people are usually very focused individuals.

If I can have undistracted time working on a project, I can complete it efficiently and quickly. But if I am distracted, I lose focus and oftentimes make mistakes, lose creative streams of thought, and am hindered in completion.

What you focus on, you empower. If you focus on your project, you will empower its successful completion. If you focus on problems you will empower the problems, but if you focus on possibilities you will empower the possibilities.

Focus is powerful. Keep a strong, undistracted focus on the areas of success you desire to embrace.

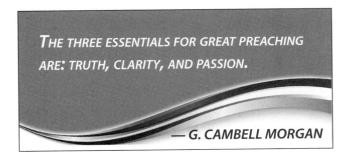

THE THREE ESSENTIALS FOR GREAT PREACHING ARE: TRUTH, CLARITY, AND PASSION.

— G. CAMBELL MORGAN

A Brilliant Plan
of Action

A well-defined desire or goal that is full of passion and focus is not enough to accomplish success. You must have a plan of action. Desire without substance is an unfulfilled dream, and faith without works is dead.

God had a desire to redeem mankind from our sinful state. This desire is clearly recorded in the Scripture, but it was not simply desire that brought fulfillment to His dream – it was His plan of action. He had a clear desire and intended outcome, a written plan of action, and timelines for each aspect to be fulfilled. God acted on His plan of action.

God gave Moses the plan to build the tabernacle in the desert. In fact, He told Moses to build it "according to

the pattern" (see Exodus 25). When Moses acted on the plan, the tabernacle was built.

Your plan of action to fulfill your dream needs to include steps of action that will accomplish your goal. This is so much fun. Think it all through. What is needed? When creating your plan of action, consider the equipment, workers, time demands, and finances (budget) that you will need to fulfill your goal, and write it down.

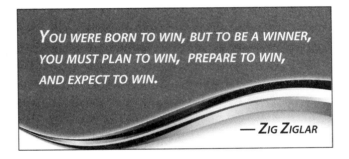

YOU WERE BORN TO WIN, BUT TO BE A WINNER, YOU MUST PLAN TO WIN, PREPARE TO WIN, AND EXPECT TO WIN.

— ZIG ZIGLAR

KEY #7

Do It!

The Bible says that faith without works is dead. I know many dear ones who have the most amazing dreams and desires. They also have great action plans to accomplish their goals, but they don't act on it. As a result, it is only talk. There is an old saying, "All talk and no action" – good, faith-filled talk is important when you are sharing the vision, but just talk will not accomplish it. Without works, it will only be a good dream and a wonderful plan.

Knowledge of a thing is not possession of it. There must be action.

The following are some keys that successful people practice:

1. **Start** – Don't just talk about your plan, do it.

2. **Diligence** – Success takes hard work and lots of it. Be diligent.

3. **Strong Start and Strong Finish** – Many like to initiate their plans but they don't finish strong. Renew your strength, passion, and focus so that you have a strong finish.

4. **Excellence** – Anything worth doing is worth doing well. Strive for excellence and quality.

5. **Work Ethics** – Integrity

6. **Teachability** – As you move forward to fulfill your goals, invite people that you trust to speak into your life. Those who have succeeded in the same field will be able to give you pointers and help you learn valuable elements to success. Be teachable.

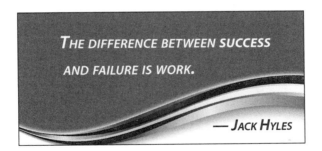

THE DIFFERENCE BETWEEN SUCCESS AND FAILURE IS WORK.

— JACK HYLES

KEY #8

SOWING AND REAPING

I love the Kingdom law of sowing and reaping. It works for all the people all the time, and it works in every area of your life.

One day I was sharing a little life lesson with my grandson and explained this law. I taught him that he would receive out of life what he sowed into it. If he wanted friends, he would need to sow friendship. If he wanted favor, he would need to sow favor. If he desired a brilliant mind, he would need to sow academics into his life (he was not too keen on that one). I demonstrated the principle of sowing and reaping through the example of a bean seed. I explained that if you want beans, you need to plant a bean seed. If you plant a corn seed you will not reap a bean. Whatever you want in life, you need to plant the seed of that desire.

God made a perpetual promise to Noah and said that as long as the earth remained there would be seedtime and a corresponding harvest. Whatever you sow you WILL reap.

> While the earth remains, seedtime and harvest, and cold and heat, and summer and winter, and day and night shall not cease.
>
> *GENESIS 8:22*

> God is not mocked; for whatever a man sows, this he will also reap.
>
> *GALATIANS 6:7*

8 FACTS ABOUT SOWING AND REAPING

1. There will be a time to sow and a time to reap a corresponding harvest.

2. Whatever you sow, you will reap.

3. The quantity of your harvest depends on how much you sow.

4. The quality of ground you sow into will determine your harvest.

5. Seeds take time to grow.

6. You will always reap more than you sow.

7. Both sowing and reaping need to be intentional.

8. The fruit of your harvest will contain more seed for sowing.

You are living in the harvest of what you sowed in days past.

If you do not like the fruit you're reaping, you can start now to sow good seed into your field of life. You WILL reap what you sow.

If your life is not producing the harvest you desire, take some time to examine your field.

"Behold, the sower went out to sow; as he was sowing, some seed fell beside the road, and the birds came and ate it up. Other seed fell on the rocky ground where it did not have much soil; and immediately it sprang up because it had no depth of soil. And after the sun had risen, it was scorched; and because it had no root, it withered away. Other seed fell among the thorns, and the thorns came up and choked it, and it yielded no crop. Other seeds fell into the good soil, and as they grew up and increased, they yielded a crop and produced thirty, sixty, and a hundredfold." And He was saying, "He who has ears to hear, let him hear."

MARK 4

The parable of the sower and the seed speaks of the ground the seed is sown into. If you sow good seed into good ground, you WILL reap a harvest. There are certain types of soil that will not produce a harvest.

Are you investing into good soil? For example, if you plan to sow your time into a person's life to help them in their personal development, you want to make sure they are willing to make changes and will diligently apply the principles they learn. If not, it is poor soil and it will not produce fruit.

THE SOWER SOWS THE WORD

The words you speak are very powerful: they can create or destroy. In the book of James it says that the course of our life is determined by the words we speak (see James 3:4-5). In Proverbs it says that we reap the fruit of our lips (see Proverbs 18:20).

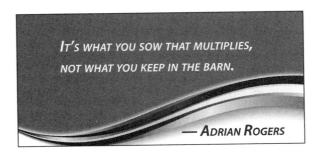

IT'S WHAT YOU SOW THAT MULTIPLIES, NOT WHAT YOU KEEP IN THE BARN.

— ADRIAN ROGERS

When you decree (proclaim) the Word of God over your life, it will produce fruit. Isaiah 55:11 says, "So shall My word be that goes forth from My mouth; it shall not return to Me void, but it shall accomplish what I please, and it shall prosper *in the thing* for which I sent it (NKJV).

Hebrews 11:3 states that "By faith ... the worlds were framed by the word of God" (NKJV). Therefore, you can frame a successful future by sowing the Word of God. Jesus said that the words He speaks are spirit and life (see John 6:63). When you speak His Word over your life, you create great blessings and success.

> This book of the law shall not depart from your mouth, but you shall meditate in it day and night, so that you may be careful to do according to all that is written in it; for then you will make your way prosperous, and then you will have success.
>
> *JOSHUA 1:8*

Deliberately sow the Word into your life, and you will succeed.

KEY #9

Endurance and Overcoming Obstacles

I do not know of a successful person who has not faced challenges. In fact, it is usually when they overcome obstacles and challenges that they are promoted. A successful person is determined to overcome any hindrance in their way. They overcome discouragement and go for it. They look upon the challenges as stepping stones to their destination.

> Let us not lose heart in doing good, for in due time we will reap if we do not grow weary.
>
> *GALATIANS 6:9*

Perspective is important. If you begin to see hardship as a tool to create success, it changes everything for you. You become empowered during the challenge rather than weakened. Leap over your hurdles and if you fall, get up and try again. This is how champions are created!

Finishing Strong

I have met many great starters who were poor finishers. Your success is not based on what you start, but on what you complete.

Begin with a small project that is realistic for you to complete short term, and then stay with it until it's finished. When you finish it, you have succeeded. That one success – as small as it might seem – will build momentum for the next one. When you feel like giving up, remember to finish strong. Successful people finish strong. Jesus did!

Any problem can be solved and any obstacle overcome.

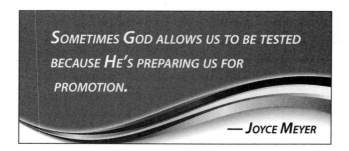

SOMETIMES GOD ALLOWS US TO BE TESTED BECAUSE HE'S PREPARING US FOR PROMOTION.

— JOYCE MEYER

KEY #10

POWERFUL ALLIANCES AND RELATIONSHIPS

Primarily, Jesus discipled His followers through relationship – He called the twelve to follow Him and, through their association with Him, they became disciples and learned to be like Him in character and nature, doing the "same works" He did. The book of Acts provides an amazing example of how powerfully the association with Jesus influenced Peter and John:

> Now as they observed the confidence of Peter and John and understood that they were uneducated and untrained men, they were amazed, and began to **recognize them as having been with Jesus**.

> ACTS 4:13, *EMPHASIS ADDED*

Associations influence your life for sure. Parents under-
stand this. If your child's friends are rebellious and disre-
spectful, then you know that your child could be headed
in that direction. On the other hand, if your child keeps
company with respectful and wise friends, you have peace
regarding their social and behavioral development. My
mother used to tell me, "You become like the company
you keep, so be careful who you associate with."

Associations have powerful impact on your life.

If you are looking to be successful in life, it is wise to evaluate your relationships and associations. We are called to
love all people all the time. Love is not an option and
love always desires the highest good for the sake of an-
other. To be truly successful in life is to learn to love well.
1 Corinthians 14:1 says, "Let love be your greatest aim."

Every relationship is a gift. Some individuals who are
brought into your life are those that you will invest in to
help build their gifts, callings, and character. Some individuals you find in your life will be wonderful grace
growers for you. These are ones that will test your love
and as a result teach you to love like Jesus in the "fel-
lowship of His sufferings" (Phil 3:10). There are others,
however, that God will bring into your life to help you
grow in areas you desire to develop and succeed in.

In my coaching course, *Keys to Success*, I take the partici-
pant through evaluations of various relationships in their

life and then invite them to strategically and intentionally build relationships that will help mentor and develop them in areas they are believing for growth and success in.

As a young Christian, I was hungry to learn about the Holy Spirit so I attended classes at my church on the gifts of the Spirit. In class, I met others who were not only hungry to grow in the Spirit, but many who were much more seasoned, mature, and familiar with spiritual things. I intentionally asked a few if I could spend some time with them after class. The more I associated with them and others who were hungry for God and the things of the Spirit, the more I grew. When we fellowshipped, we shared testimonies and insights with each other about what we had learned and experienced. A realm of anointing in exercising gifts of the Spirit grew and expanded through this group of people. It spread throughout our congregation until many in our church came to believe in and enjoy the benefits of God's supernatural power and the flow of the spiritual gifts. Our church became known as a place where the Spirit of God moved, and I became seasoned as a minister of the Spirit through the help of those God-designed relationships.

You can strategically choose relationships in order to grow or succeed in an area. For example, if you desire to grow in your entrepreneurial skills, it would not be beneficial to receive counsel, input, or influence from those who have a history of failure. You can and should intentionally build associations that will empower you as a budding entrepreneur. Even if you do not know anyone personally, in today's world of media you can receive mentoring and instruction through online seminars and workshops. There are successful authors, instructors, and counselors in the field of business who can guide you and help you develop through their resources.

I have also discovered that hiring a Life Coach who is seasoned in the area you desire to grow in is very powerful and beneficial for personal development. A good coach will help you to see blind spots, examine options, and come to points of breakthrough. The one-on-one relationship with a coach can accelerate your development through the intense and concentrated focus the experience offers.

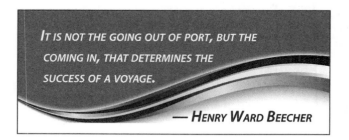

IT IS NOT THE GOING OUT OF PORT, BUT THE COMING IN, THAT DETERMINES THE SUCCESS OF A VOYAGE.

— HENRY WARD BEECHER

FINAL WORDS OF ENCOURAGEMENT FOR YOU

Beloved, YOU were created for success. God is so committed to your success that He sent His only begotten Son to die on the cross for you and to take care of all your failures and shortcomings.

He wants to break any and all cycles and patterns of defeat that have plagued your life. You are called to manifest His goodness in every area of your life. This is YOUR GIFT from HIM!

It might be helpful to examine past failures and invite the Lord to show you the elements and dynamics that produced them, but you cannot live in remorse of the past. Look to the goodness of God. Expect His goodness to manifest. Turn a corner in your life and step into a life filled with success that will never end.

Feel free to pray the following prayer:

> Jesus, thank You for paying the price for my freedom from sin and failure. Thank You for giving me Your success as a gift. I choose to receive this gift in fullness. I receive Your goodness. I receive Your love. I receive the gift of breakthrough You grant me this day! Fill me to overflowing with Your Spirit and Your grace, that I might become a sweet aroma of Your presence in every place I walk in life. Thank You, Jesus.

Now, GO and succeed!

> "Every place on which the sole of your foot treads, I have given it to you."
>
> **JOSHUA 1:3**

> "Be strong and courageous! Do not tremble or be dismayed, for the Lord your God is with you wherever you go."
>
> **JOSHUA 1:9**

Appendix

INSPIRING QUOTES

Some people dream of great accomplishments, while others stay awake and do them.
— ANONYMOUS

It is not the going out of port, but the coming in, that determines the **success** of a voyage.
— HENRY WARD BEECHER

The **success** or failure of our work as a church or mission depends, in the last resort, largely, not in the number of preachers we put into the field, nor on the size of our congregations, but rather on the character of Christianity we and our work produce.
— DUNCAN CAMPBELL

Love is **success**, Love is happiness, Love is life. God is Love. Therefore LOVE. — HENRY DRUMMOND

Picture yourself vividly as winning, and that alone will contribute immeasurably to **success**.
— HARRY EMERSON FOSDICK

Without continual growth and progress, such words as improvement, achievement, and **success** have no meaning. — BENJAMIN FRANKLIN

Your **success** and happiness lies in you. Resolve to keep happy, and your joy and you shall form an invincible host against difficulties.
— HELEN KELLER

Failure defeats losers, failure inspires winners.
— ROBERT T. KIYOSAKI

Success is getting what you want; happiness wants what you get. — WOODROW KROLL

Those who have failed miserably are often the first to see God's formula for **success**. — EDWIN LUTZER

Now, as old Dr. Bonner of Glasgow said, "The Lord didn't show Joshua how to use the sword, but He told him how he should meditate on the Lord day and night, and then he would have good **success**."
— **D. L. Moody**

To court apparent **success** by merely whipping up people's enthusiasm results in a work without God.
— **Watchman Nee**

I attribute my **success** to this – I never gave or took any excuse. — **Florence Nightingale**

That action is not warrantable which either fears to ask the divine blessing on its performance, or having succeeded, does not come with thanksgiving to God for its **success**. — **Francis Quaries**

Success is the world's criterion of merit; fidelity is God's. — **Charles Robinson**

His authority on earth allows us to dare to go to all the nations. His authority in heaven gives us our only hope of **success**. And His presence with us leaves us no other choice. — **John Stott**

Discipline is the soul of an army. It makes small numbers formidable; procures **success** to the weak, and esteem to all. — GEORGE WASHINGTON

My mother was the most beautiful woman I ever saw. All I am I owe to my mother. I attribute all my **success** in life to the moral, intellectual and physical education I received from her.
— GEORGE WASHINGTON

If your ship doesn't come in, swim out to meet it!
— JONATHAN WINTERS

Success is dependent upon the glands – sweat glands.
— ZIG ZIGLAR

The foundation stones for a balanced **success** are honesty, character, integrity, faith, love and loyalty.
— ZIG ZIGLAR

You cannot climb the ladder of **success** dressed in the costume of failure. — ZIG ZIGLAR

Sometimes adversity is what you need to face in order to become **successful**. — ZIG ZIGLAR

About Patricia King

For over thirty years, Patricia has success-
fully coached, trained, and equipped believers to walk in their
God-given callings. She has encouraged thousands through
her prophetic ministry to see their potential in Christ and
has walked through many challenging situations into glorious victory.

As a seasoned minister, businesswoman, and popular moti-
vational speaker, Patricia King is the author of many books
and resources, host of *Everlasting Love* TV program, and
founder and visionary of XP Ministries.

Her passion in life is to empower others to fulfill their
dreams, visions, and desires and to help those who are strug-
gling to experience their breakthroughs. She is a skilled com-
municator and a gifted coach. Prophetic encouragement and
ministry uniquely mark Patricia's coaching sessions.

For more information about her life coaching seminars,
webinars, one-on-one coaching and group workshops, visit
her page at patriciakinglifecoach.com.

For more information about XP Ministries, go to XPmin-
istries.com.

Watch Patricia King's video teachings and television pro-
grams on XPmedia.com.

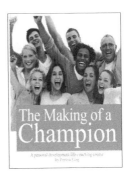
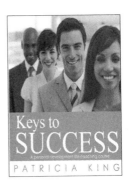

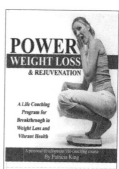

STEP INTO THE BLESSING ZONE!

You were created to be blessed, to know the very best that God has to offer all the days of your life. If you have been living in a place of lack, hardship, or frustration, it is time to shift into the Blessing Zone and know the goodness of God in every area of your life!

In this powerful book, Patricia King shares divine secrets of how you can step out of simply living day-to-day, and live IN THE ZONE!

THE VOICE OF WISDOM

Compiled by Patricia King, this inspiring modern day paraphrase of the Book of Proverbs is full of practical and eternal wisdom that is easy to comprehend, receive, and apply to your life. You will uncover the mysteries of maximized living, written in words and expressions that make sense to people of our day. Learn how to have a happy, successful life that is pleasing to the Lord, and get the answers to every question you could possibly have.

ARE YOU READY TO SOAR?

Do you long for deeper experiences with God? Would you like to press in for a more intimate relationship with Him? Well, He is longing for the same with you!

The *Glory School* builds Scripture upon Scripture to guide you deep into the reality of God and His divine Kingdom. You will receive insight and impartation that strengthens your faith and deepens your relationship with the Lord.

You will learn how you can experience the angelic realm, the third heaven, and closer encounters with the Holy Spirit. Get ready to experience the Lord in completely new levels of revelation and intimacy!

New! All 18 lessons in MP3 format and the manual on a USB stick (flash drive). It is also available on CD, MP3 and DVD, and can be ordered along with the manual or separately.

Additional copies of this book, other
book titles and coaching resources
by Patricia King are available at:
patriciakinglifecoach.com
and XPministries.com

Wholesale prices for stores
and ministries

Please contact:
usaresource@xpministries.com.

Most XP Publishing books are also available to
wholesale and retail stores through
anchordistributors.com

www.XPpublishing.com
XP Ministries